HOLISTIC
PLAN OF CARE

PARENTING WORKBOOK

Dr. Barbara Thomas-Reddick, PhD, CAP

To order additional copies of this book, contact:
Xlibris
844-714-8691
www.Xlibris.com
Orders@Xlibris.com

ISBN: Softcover   979-8-3694-0272-6
               EBook   979-8-3694-0271-9

Print information available on the last page

Rev. date: 07/10/2023

Parenting style can affect everything from your child's self-esteem and physical health to how they relate to others. It is important to ensure your parenting style is supporting healthy growth and development because the way you interact with your child and how you discipline them will influence them for the rest of their life. Diana Baumrind, a developmental psychologist and Dr. Barbara Thomas-Reddick, an Ordained Pastor, Certified Addiction Professional, and a Parent/Grandmother have identified several types of parenting styles.

This parenting workbook will hopefully allow you to dig deep from your childhood to present and identify ways that you could hopefully redirect ways and behavior to connect the dots in your life.

Connecting dots, could simply mean, asking the question "Who am I"? Who am I can allow one to look at one's life in the past, present, and future. Dr. Reddick's methodology is, "When we know where we have been and realize what has happened, we can then identify where we are now, and move forward to understand where I would like become or be". To become is to have a better understanding of **who** I would like to be, **what** I would like to be, and **when and how** I want to arrive there.

FOUR PARENTING STYLES

AUTHORITARIAN

CONTROLLER

Authoritarian Parenting

Are you familiar with any of these?
- You believe kids should be seen and not heard.
- When it comes to rules, you believe it's "my way or the highway."
- You don't take your child's feelings into consideration.

If any of those appear true, you might be an authoritarian/Controlling parent. Authoritarian/Controlling parents believe kids should follow the rules without exception.

Authoritarian parents are famous for saying, "Because I said so," when a child questions the reasons behind a rule. They are not interested in negotiating and their focus is on obedience. They also don't allow kids to get involved in problem-solving challenges or obstacles. However, they make rules and regulations and enforce the consequences with little regard for a child›s thoughts, concerns, or opinions.

Authoritarian parents may use punishments instead of discipline. So, rather than teach a child how to make better choices, they're invested in making kids feel sorry for their mistakes. Children who grow up with strict authoritarian parents tend to follow rules much of the time. But their obedience comes at a costly price.

Children of authoritarian parents are at a higher risk of developing self-esteem problems because their opinions aren't valued. When a child feels they are not valued, usually this child may have self-esteem issues, grades usually drop, and sometimes become isolated from their peers.

They may also become hostile and very aggressive and angry. This behavior most times the child may act out and not realize the negative behavior that may be forthcoming. Rather than think about how to do things better in the future, they often focus on the anger they feel toward their parents or themselves for not living up to parental expectations and sometimes might not have a clear understanding of what the expectation is the parent is wanting. Since authoritarian parents are often strict, their children may grow to stretch the truth or become good liars to avoid punishment.

Warning Signs that a parent may be too strict:

Zero-Tolerance Policy

While it's important to have clear rules, it's equally important to recognize that there are always exceptions to the rules. Rather than taking an authoritarian stance on everything, show a willingness to evaluate your child's behavior in the context of the circumstance.

Child Lies a Lot

While it's normal for kids to stretch the truth sometimes, research is clear that harsh discipline turns kids into good liars. If you're too strict, a child will more than likely lie to avoid punishment.

Your Child has more restrictions than other Kids:

There's nothing wrong with having different rules than the other parents. But, if you're always the strictest parent in the crowd, it could be a sign that your expectations are a bit too high.

Little Patience for Non-Sense

Most kids love ridiculous jokes and silly games. And while those jokes can get old fast, and silly behavior can slow you down, it's important to savor the moment and have fun sometimes.

Don't Respect others way of Parenting.

Strict parents often have difficulty tolerating everything from the way a teacher runs a classroom to the way Grandma handles behavior problems. It's OK for kids to be exposed to adults who have different rules and types of discipline.

The Rule list is Long.

Rules are good, but too many rules can be harmful. Keep your rules simple and only include the most important ones that you want your child to remember. Post your list of household rules in a place where you can refer to it as needed.

Child has small amount of time for Fun:

Many children with strict parents run from activity to activity with little downtime. While some structure is essential, it's also important for kids to have free time.

Natural Consequences are second to none.

Strict parents often go to great lengths to avoid letting a child make a mistake. But kids are often capable of learning from their mistakes when they face consequences that are natural.

You Nag a Lot

Nagging prevents kids from taking responsibility for their own behavior. If you find yourself nagging your child about everything from when to do their homework to when they should practice playing the piano, they won't learn to do those things on their own.

Continuously giving directions out

If you're always saying things like, "Sit up straight," "Quit dragging your feet," and "Don't slurp your drink," your child will tune you out. Save your instructions for the most important issues so your voice will be heard.

Choices are not up for discussion.

Rather than ask, "Would you rather put your clothes away first or make your bed?" Strict parents often bark over orders. Giving kids a little freedom, especially when both choices are good ones, can go a long way to gaining compliance.

Child never allowed to make decisions in the matter

Sometimes strict parents insist children do everything a certain way. They insist on making the bed the "right way" or playing with the dollhouse "appropriately." While there are times that kids need adult instruction, it's important to allow for flexibility and creativity.

Praise of Outcome is high on the scale and never Effort.

Strict parents usually don't offer a lot of praise. They reserve their affirmations for perfection, rather than effort. If you only praise your child for getting 100 on a test, or for scoring the most goals in the game, your child may think your love is conditional on high achievement.

Outrageous Threats

While most parents are guilty of making an over-the-top threat occasionally, strict parents make outrageous threats on a regular basis. They often say things like, "Clean up your room right now or I'm throwing all your toys in the trash!" Avoid making threats that you aren't prepared to follow through with and make sure consequences are about disciplining, not punishing your child.

Learning is always the Goal.

Strict parents often turn every activity into a mandatory lesson of some kind. Kids can't color a picture without being quizzed on their colors, or they can't play with a dollhouse unless they're constantly reminded of proper furniture placement. Play itself gives an opportunity for imagination and creativity and can be a great escape from the normal structure and routine.[5]

Researchers and Dr. Reddick have found kids who have authoritative parents are most likely to become responsible adults who feel comfortable self-advocating and expressing their opinions and feelings.

Children raised with authoritative discipline tend to be happy and successful. They're also more likely to be good at making sound decisions and evaluating safety risks on their own.

AUTHORITATIVE

Mother Hen

In this parenting style, **the parents are nurturing, caring and more like the mother hen, responsive, sensitive, forthcoming, and understanding, caring, helpful yet set firm limits for their children.** They attempt to control children's behavior by explaining rules, discussing, and reasoning. They listen to a child's viewpoint but don't always accept it.

Statements that may sound like you.
- You put a lot of effort into creating and maintaining a positive relationship with your child.
- You explain the reasons behind your rules.
- You set limits, enforce rules, and give consequences, but take your child's feelings into consideration.

If those statements sound familiar, you may be an authoritative parent. Authoritative parents have rules, and they use consequences, but they also take their children's opinions into account. They validate their children's feelings, while also making it clear that the adults are ultimately in charge. This is the approach backed by research and experts as the most developmentally healthy and effective parenting style.

Authoritative parents invest time and energy into preventing behavior problems before they start. They also use positive discipline strategies to reinforce positive behavior, like praise and incentives.

Researchers have found kids who have authoritative parents are most likely to become responsible adults who feel comfortable self-advocating and expressing their opinions and feelings.

Children raised with authoritative discipline tend to be happy and successful. They're also more likely to be good at making sound decisions and evaluating safety risks on their own.

Welfare of Authoritative Parenting

Out of all the parenting styles, children who are raised with an authoritative style of parenting have been shown to exhibit the best outcomes. Some of the many benefits of this approach for kids include the following:

- They are more compassionate, caring and warm.
- They may be more resistant to peer pressure.
- They become more responsible, can regulate themselves, and learn to make good decisions on their own.
- They have respect for adults, other people, and rules.
- They tend to have fewer social problems with peers, get along with teachers, and be more socially accepted at school.
- They tend to have secure attachments and better relationships with their parents.
- They're not anxious or worried about who's in charge because they know who is making decisions to make sure they are healthy and happy: the parents.

PASSIVE

UNASSERTIVE

What sounds familiar to you?
- You set rules but rarely enforce them.
- You don't give out consequences very often.
- You think your child will learn best with little interference from you.

If those statements sound familiar, you might be a permissive parent. Permissive parents are lenient. They often only step in when there's a serious problem.

They're quite forgiving, and they adopt an attitude of "kids will be kids." When they do use consequences, they may not make those consequences stick. They might give privileges back if a child begs or they may allow a child to get out of time-out early if they promise to be good.

Permissive parents usually take on more of a friend role than a parent role. They often encourage their children to talk with them about their problems, but they usually don't put much effort into discouraging poor choices or bad behavior.[4]

Kids who grow up with permissive parents are more likely to struggle academically.

They may exhibit more behavioral problems as they don't appreciate authority and rules. They often have low self-esteem and may report a lot of sadness.

They're also at a higher risk for health problems, like obesity, because permissive parents struggle to limit unhealthy food intake or promote regular exercise or healthy sleep habits. They are even more likely to have dental cavities because permissive parents often don't enforce good habits, like ensuring a child brushes their teeth.

UNINVOLVED
ABSENT

Do any of these statements sound familiar?
- You don't ask your child about school or homework.
- You rarely know where your child is or who they are with.
- You don't spend much time with your child.

If those statements sound familiar, you might be an uninvolved parent. Uninvolved parents tend to have little knowledge of what their children are doing. There tend to be few rules in the household. Children may not receive much guidance, nurturing, and parenthood.

Uninvolved parents expect children to raise themselves. They don't devote much time or energy into meeting children's basic needs. Uninvolved parents may be neglectful but it's not always intentional. A parent with mental health issues or substance abuse problems, for example, may not be able to care for a child's physical or emotional needs on a consistent basis.

At other times, uninvolved parents lack knowledge about child development—or they may believe that their child will do better without their oversight. And sometimes, they're simply overwhelmed with other problems, like work, paying bills, and managing a household.

Children with uninvolved parents are likely to struggle with self-esteem issues.

They tend to perform poorly in school. They also exhibit frequent behavior problems and rank low in happiness.

IDENTIFY WHICH PARENTING STYLE YOU ARE:

1. **AUTHORITARIAN** (Controller) _____

2. **AUTHORITATIVE** (Mother Hen) _____

3. **UNINVOLVED** (Absent) _____

4. **PASSIVE** (Unassertive) _____

PARENT ASSESSMENT

1. **Parents should provide direction but also listen to and discuss their kids' concerns. (Check one)**
   a. Agree _____
   b. Strongly Agree _____
   c. Do not Agree _____

2. **Kids should make most of their own decisions without parental direction. (Check one)**
   a. Agree _____
   b. Strongly Agree _____
   c. Do not Agree _____

3. **There shouldn't be rigid rules for kids' behavior. (Check one)**
   a. Agree _____
   b. Strongly Agree _____
   c. Do not Agree _____

4. **Parents should provide direction and guidance in rational and objective ways. (Check one)**
   a. Agree _____
   b. Strongly Agree _____
   c. Do not Agree _____

5. **Children should be told exactly what to do and how to do it. (Check one)**
   a. Agree _____
   b. Strongly Agree _____
   c. Do not Agree _____

6. **Kids can make up their own minds and do what they want to do. (Check one)**

a. Agree _____

b. Strongly Agree _____

c. Do not Agree _____

7. **Kids need to learn early on who the boss is in the family. (Check one)**

a. Agree _____

b. Strongly Agree _____

c. Do not Agree _____

8. **Children should get their way as often as the parents do. (Check one)**

a. Agree _____

b. Strongly Agree _____

c. Do not Agree _____

9. **Parents should discuss the reasons behind their policies with their children. (Check one)**

a. Agree _____

b. Strongly Agree _____

c. Do not Agree _____

10. **Children should follow their parents' orders without asking questions. (Check one)**

a. Agree _____

b. Strongly Agree _____

c. Do not Agree _____

11. **Parents should make their expectations of their children very clear and open to discussion. (Check one)**

a. Agree _____

b. Strongly Agree _____

c. Do not Agree _____

12. Parents shouldn't restrict children's activities or decisions. (Check one)

    a. Agree _____

    b. Strongly Agree _____

    c. Do not Agree _____

13. Children shouldn't conform to what parents know is right. (Check one)

    a. Agree _____

    b. Strongly Agree _____

    c. Do not Agree _____

14. Children should be encouraged to discuss family rules and restrictions. (Check one)

    a. Agree _____

    b. Strongly Agree _____

    c. Do not Agree _____

COUNT YOUR ANSWERS:

TOTAL AGREE _____

TOTAL STRONGLY AGREE _____

TOTAL DO NOT AGREE _____

Breakdown of Dysfunctional Family Roles

Most experts identify six dysfunctional family roles in particular. In these books, *Another Chance: Hope and Health for the Alcoholic Family*, addiction and codependency expert Sharon Wegscheider-Cruse identifies the six dysfunctional family roles of the alcoholic family as follows:

- The Dependent
- The Enabler
- The Hero
- The Scapegoat
- The Lost Child
- The Mascot

Wherever you go for information on alcoholic family dysfunction, you will usually see these roles listed. Dysfunctional family dynamics, however, arise from more than just addiction. For instance, the six roles attributed to a family torn apart by divorce or separation look slightly different from those above. The Scapegoat only exists as a variant of another role dubbed the Problem Child, with the Enabler renamed as the Caretaker. Naturally, the Dependent occupies no place in such a family. And even in some cases of families affected by one member's drug use, the Dependent simply occupies the Problem Child role, leaving space for another category known as the Mastermind.

If that all sounds a bit confusing, don't worry. We do not expect you to accept just one model of dysfunctional family dynamics. Again, every family works differently. Furthermore, many children or other family members may fit into multiple categories. The Hero may sometimes feel like a Lost Child, and the Mascot (also known as the Family Clown) sometimes becomes the Scapegoat. In many cases, the Dependent may fit into multiple roles as well—especially in families involving more than one substance user.

While we usually see these roles attributed to children, they do not simply vanish upon reaching adulthood. Those who grew up in alcoholic or addicted families may wear these masks for the rest of their lives. Licensed counselor and social worker Sharon Martin discusses why this happens, using <u>adult children of alcoholics</u> as an example:

"Children crave and need predictability. Your needs must be met consistently in order for you to feel safe and develop secure attachments. This didn't happen in your dysfunctional family. Alcoholic families are in 'survival mode.' Usually everyone is tiptoeing around the alcoholic, trying to keep the peace and avoid a blow up."

Failure to develop secure attachments can result in any of the dysfunctional family roles listed. Looking past the traditional six roles and embracing all eight discussed above, allows us to dive deeper into this issue. Whether you are a Dependent, an Enabler, or any mix of roles discussed, identifying the effects of family dysfunction on your own behaviors will mark the first step on the road to healing.

The Dependent

We generally characterize the Dependent as the focal point within the greater spectrum of dysfunctional family roles. As they slide farther down the scale and lose themselves to substance abuse, the family's trajectory alters course. Family members change their behaviors, whether willingly or unwillingly, to accommodate the Dependent's lifestyle. For some, this means enabling. A family member may find themselves lying to family friends or cancelling obligations to bail their loved one out of a jam. Other family members react more harshly, sometimes even cutting off all contact with the Dependent. At either extreme, this changes the whole of the family dynamic.

Naturally, the Dependent faces the most obvious struggles in recovery. In fact, some might even say they benefit from the existence of such a clear-cut role. They often needn't do much soul-searching to arrive at the conclusion that their behaviors must change. (Obviously, there are exceptions, and not all Dependents succeed in recovery or even attempt it.) The Dependent will still need to identify certain behavior patterns if they wish to achieve a full recovery. At the onset, however, the problematic aspects of this dysfunction will appear far more tangibly than those stemming from other dysfunctional family roles.

The Caretaker

Also known as the Enabler, we can identify at least one primary similarity between the Caretaker and the Dependent: the bulk of their daily lives seem to revolve around drugs and alcohol.

Common behaviors of the Caretaker may include posting bail after an arrest, making excuses for their addicted loved one's behavior, and looking after the Dependent's basic needs when intoxication prevents the Dependent from doing so themselves. Caretakers generally suffer from codependency, which affects their relationships with all members of the household. They often facilitate—and sometimes encourage, whether purposefully or not—all dysfunctional family roles. Heaping praise upon the Hero, enabling the Problem Child's behaviors, falling prey to the Mastermind's manipulation, etc.

We usually think of the Caretaker as a spouse or parent. In some cases, however, the chemical dependency of an adult in the household may necessitate that one of the children step up to fill this role. In such cases, the Caretaker may fit the roles of both Hero and Lost Child. They work to keep the family together but grow up feeling as if they never got to experience a true childhood. This may lead to feelings of bitterness and resentment. Fear and inadequacy also tend to characterize the Caretaker, especially those who blame themselves for the Dependent's suffering.

The Problem Child

You do not often see the Problem Child on the roster of dysfunctional family roles as they pertain to addiction. Perhaps one explanation for this might be the assumption that the Problem Child and the Dependent are usually one and the same. Indeed, one particularly rebellious child sometimes influences the whole of the family dynamic, leading the rest of the household to respond by filling the rest of the categories. And as one may presume, this rebellion does often include the use of drugs and alcohol.

However, the Problem Child may also arise in response to the dysfunction caused by a Dependent. Sometimes a Lost Child becomes tired of feeling neglected and decides to act out. In some cases, the Problem Child acts as an inadvertent Caretaker, enabling the Dependent by diverting attention onto their own misbehavior. Occasionally, though not necessarily in most cases, diversion may even act as the Problem Child's primary intention. The latter case presents us with a rare example of a time in which the Problem Child will also play the role of Hero, depending upon which family member's viewpoint we apply to their behavior.

Most experts in addiction and family dysfunction apply this description to the Scapegoat. This would make our inclusion of the Problem Child appear redundant. But as you will see below, we might make at least one important distinction between these two seemingly identical dysfunctional family roles.

The Scapegoat

Many define the Scapegoat in the same manner as we defined the Problem Child above, particularly regarding those who draw attention away from the Dependent's behavior. They characterize this as an effort to protect their addicted family members, possibly out of feelings of guilt or shame. But in *Not My Kid: A Family's Guide to Kids and Drugs*—which precedes Wegscheider-Cruse's book by about five years—authors Beth Polson and Dr. Miller Newton define the Scapegoat as a family member who often does nothing to earn their role within the family's dysfunction.

In this take on dysfunctional family roles, the Scapegoat suffers misplaced blame for the behaviors of others in the family. Rather than a Problem Child who diverts attention, this definition casts the Scapegoat as an individual who generally exhibits relative stability and emotional health compared to the rest of the household. Nonetheless, they may receive blame for the Dependent's behaviors if even tangentially connected to them. "How could you allow this to happen?" "Why didn't you say something sooner?" In some cases, they may even receive blame for events in which they did not participate by any action or inaction, and in fact did not even know about until they found themselves drawn into the conflict as a wrongly accused culprit.

The Scapegoat will sometimes grow to believe others' perceptions of them. The guilt with which they have been unjustly saddled will characterize future relationships by causing frequent feelings of inferiority and self-loathing.

By contrast, some Scapegoats who recognize their unfair treatment may struggle with trust issues. And due to the complexities of human behavior, some Scapegoats will find themselves regularly torn between both extremes.

The Mastermind

Much like the Problem Child, the Mastermind may fail to appear on most addiction-centered breakdowns of dysfunctional family roles due to the sheer assumption that the Dependent usually takes up this mantle. We associate the Mastermind with manipulation and opportunism, traits sometimes employed by Dependents to hide or facilitate their continued use. From the standpoint of the Caretaker, and occasionally the Scapegoat, the Dependent most certainly fills this role.

The Mastermind, however, sometimes occupies a much more complex space within the overall family dynamic. Some Masterminds put on the façade of other dysfunctional family roles at will, depending upon the aims they seek to achieve. Usually, however, the Mastermind simply observes the behaviors exhibited by the rest of the family, using them to their advantage. They may use the diversions of the Problem Child or Scapegoat to engage in their own misbehavior. Or they may take advantage of the Caretaker's enabling nature to fulfill desires that might otherwise be denied to them.

We should clarify that, while the above description casts the Mastermind almost as a villain, they don't necessarily act with nefarious intent. Sometimes, in the wake of the chaos caused by competing dysfunctional family roles, opportunism may seem the only way to meet their needs.

Take, for instance, a child who provides emotional support to a Caretaker simply to receive affection in return. This act fits the Mastermind role, as their intention revolves around their own emotional well-being rather than the Caretaker's. But, while perhaps opportunistic, the behavior is still quite understandable. All dysfunctional family roles, when broken down to their core, are merely different ways of seeking validation, or attention. The need itself is not symptomatic of dysfunction, but rather a fundamental part of human nature. It is only the behavior used to fulfill this need that we may call dysfunctional.

The Hero

The Caretaker might make excuses for the Dependent, but the Hero is ultimately the one who does the best job of bringing esteem to the family. Heroes work hard to demonstrate responsibility, seeking achievement in any form possible. Younger Heroes will often find numerous extracurricular activities at school, while working in their free time. The family may rarely see the Hero due to the sheer amount of time they spend adding to their roster of accomplishments.

Despite outward appearances, the Hero suffers as much internal strife as any of the other dysfunctional family roles. Due to their hard-working lifestyle and extreme perfectionism, Heroes suffer high levels of stress. The constant struggle for achievement, the drive to set themselves apart from the family's dysfunction, essentially becomes its own addiction. Much like the Caretaker, the Hero often develops major control issues. They seek validation by trying to control the world around them. To some extent, they may succeed in this. But as each accomplishment fails to provide true inner peace, they respond by working even harder. Eventually, the Hero may take on too much or spread themselves too thin. This leads to extreme feelings of guilt and shame when the Hero finally takes on a task they cannot accomplish and must come to grips with failure.

Relationships between the Hero and other family members sometimes become volatile. The Hero may resent the Dependent or Problem Child, blaming them for the family's struggles. They may even blame the Caretaker for allowing this to happen. In many cases, the Hero feels stuck in their lifestyle simply because nobody else is stepping up to the plate. They may feel as if the family's burdens rest upon their shoulders. Left unresolved, these inflated feelings of self-importance may lead to a difficult life of constant overwork.

The Mascot

All the dysfunctional family roles share one thing in common—regardless of their outlook on the situation, they usually take the Dependent's addiction seriously. The same can be said of the Mascot; however, you wouldn't necessarily know it upon first glance.

The Mascot often cracks jokes or finds other ways of trying to provide entertainment. They do so in an attempt to alleviate the family's stress, although sometimes this may backfire. Particularly insensitive jokes or immature antics will sometimes test others' patience. When their jokes are poorly received, this often only heightens their fear and causes them to double down with more humor. On such occasions, the Mascot may briefly switch roles and become the Scapegoat. Eventually, when things calm down, they return to their role as the family jester.

Much like the Hero, the Mascot's outward appearance masks deep-seated insecurities. They use their sense of humor as a defense mechanism to put off dealing with pain, fear, or any other sort of emotional discomfort that might cause them trouble. As a result, these feelings remain unprocessed and unresolved. Mascots find themselves in a state of arrested emotional development, unable to cope properly with negative emotions. Their sense of humor becomes their most defining characteristic, and they fear that any failure on their part to maintain it may result in abandonment. And so while their antics may gain them some popularity (both inside and outside the family), this popularity feels cheap. The Mascot becomes isolated within a sea of people who enjoy their company, yet don't really know them as anything other than a walking laugh factory.

The Lost Child

Each of the above dysfunctional family roles manifests through action. The Lost Child stands apart, in that we characterize this role primarily by inaction. Those who fit into this role try hard not to rock the boat. They may never mention the Dependent's behavior, perhaps even going out of their way to avoid family discussions about it. Introverted and inconspicuous, the Lost Child may take this role by choice. Many times, however, the Lost Child is as their title implies—someone whose needs were simply neglected, lost in the bedlam of family drama.

Since we characterize the Lost Child by their neglected needs, they may easily fit into many of the other dysfunctional family roles. A Lost Child who gets fed up and angry with their role may wear the mask of Problem Child for a day, simply to take the spotlight for a short period of time. The Hero may identify as the Lost Child if they feel the rest of the family does not acknowledge their achievements. Sometimes the Lost Child plays the role of Scapegoat, disappearing from the family's radar until they become entangled in a family dispute against their will. Usually, however, the Lost Child simply stays out of the way. In a dysfunctional household, the Lost Child feels it safer to remain neither seen nor heard.

Even when the Lost Child assumes their role by choice, they may still resent the family for their neglect. Lost Children often grow up feeling ostracized, lonely and inadequate. They assume their neglect must result from some sort of personal failing. That something must be wrong with them, or else they would receive the love they deserve. This lack of esteem may lead to dangerous behaviors later, such as self-harm or a tendency to become involved in abusive relationships.

Overcoming Family Dysfunction

We think of addiction as tearing families apart. Fearing the worst, those who find themselves struggling with addiction in the household may resign themselves to fate.

"I cannot save this person."

"Things will never change."

"Our family deserved a better life."

These defeatist thoughts, while quite understandable, find little basis. Yes, many families do find themselves torn asunder due to addiction. But it doesn't have to be this way. Do you know the single easiest way to tell that the hypothetical speakers above are lying to themselves? None of them speak to the present. The first two+ offer bleak prophesies of the future, while the other mistakes their present situation for a history already written.

In the present, right now, an opportunity lies before you. If you were able to recognize yourself in any of the dysfunctional family roles above, then you have already taken an amazing step toward personal growth.

The healing process usually begins when the Dependent enters recovery. In our programs, we allow the family to involve themselves in their loved one's care. They can speak with our therapists, check in on progress. Families may arrange calls with the therapist and their loved one to discuss their differences and resolve issues within the family dynamic. This helps them to begin overcoming their dysfunctional family roles. In a sense, the entire family enters recovery simultaneously.

Family members may take other steps toward recovery in their own time as well. Support groups such as Al-Anon, Nar-Anon, Codependents Anonymous and Adult Children of Alcoholics provide a forum for families to share about their dysfunctional family roles and how addiction has impacted their lives. Working with a therapist, engaging in the Dependent's recovery and building your own support network will take you a long way toward overcoming family dysfunction. Recovery is a lifelong journey, but these steps will help you make a start. And sometimes, a good start is all you really need to begin the process that will change your life forever.

For more information on our programs and how you can help your addicted loved one while also helping yourself, contact us today for more information. We understand your pain, and we are here to help you begin moving past it.

Identify your role in the dysfunctional family and if you can place other members in the family in their role as well.

The Dependent _____

The Enabler _____

The Hero _____

The Scapegoat _____

The Lost Child _____

The Mascot _____

Mental Health: Mental health includes our emotional, psychological, and social well-being. It affects how we think, feel, and act. It also helps determine how we handle stress, relate to others, and make healthy choices. Mental health is important at every stage of life, from childhood and adolescence through adulthood.

Mental health is important because it can help you to:

- Cope with the stresses of life.
- Be physically healthy.
- Have good relationships.
- Make meaningful contributions to your community.
- Work productively.
- Realize your full potential.

Cope with stresses of life

Name one stressor you are dealing with currently.

_____

_____

_____

_____

Name and explain what it is:

_____

_____

_____

_____

_____

_____

_____

Explain how you are coping with it:

_____

_____

_____

_____

Is it someone you are angry with? If it is, how are you trying to make amends with this individual? Do you want to make amends with this person? If not, why not?

_____

_____

_____

_____

_____

_____

_____

_____

_____

BE PHYSICALLY HEALTHY

When was the last time you had a wells checkup?
_____this year _____last year _____ two years ago _____don't know.

If you haven't had a check up in a while, stop and consider scheduling a checkup with your primary care doctor. If you do not have one, try to find a doctor you feel comfortable with.

Write down the doctor you chose: _____
(THIS WILL BE A PART OF YOUR EXIT)

GREAT JOB SCHEDULING YOUR DOCTOR'S APPOINTMENT!!!!!

HAVE GOOD RELATIONSHIPS

RESPECT*********TRUST***************AFFECTION**

Respect in the relationship means that you both hold each other in high regard. When you respect someone, you admire them for certain qualities they possess and/or the character they embody.

Trust in each other means you take each other at your word. If one person says they're going to do something, the other person assumes they'll do as they say. If someone makes a mistake, the other person expects them to be honest and tell them. In fact, just comes down to each person being completely honest with the other, even when it's uncomfortable.

Affection in healthy relationships is freely given and received. Healthy couples don't need to remind themselves to show their partner that they love and appreciate them. They just do.

MAKING MEANINGFUL CONTRIBUTIONS TO YOUR COMMUNITY

In the past, identify ways you have contributed to the community.

1._____

2._____

3._____

Moving forward, identify ways you intend to contribute to the community.

1._____

2._____

3._____

4._____

Do you feel you have something to contribute to the community. If so, write them down.

1._____

2._____

3._____

<u>Work productively</u>

Are you working productively:

a. Yes _____ Explain how you are working productively?

_____

_____

b. No _____ What is keeping you from working productively?

_____

_____

<u>REALIZE YOUR FULL POTENTIAL</u>

What do you intend to achieve in life?

_____

_____

Explain your plan for reaching this achievement?

_____

_____

How can our Holistic Plan of Care Team help you achieve this achievement?

_____

_____

POWERFUL QUOTE FOR MENTAL HEALTH

"Being able to look at yourself in the mirror and identifying who you are is one of the strongest components of good mental health." All stress, anxiety, and depression are because we ignore who we are and start living to please others. To maintain wellbeing, individuals need to recognize their inner strengths."

<u>Short Mental Health Quotes</u>

What we think, we become--------Buddha

All limitations are self-imposed------Oliver Wendall Holmes

Tough times never last but tough people do--------Robert H. Schuller

What consumes your mind controls your life-------Unknown

And still, I rise-------Maya Angelou

Turn your wounds into wisdom-------------Oprah Winfrey

Persist and resist-----Epictetus

Change what you can, manage what you can't----Raymond McCauley

If you're going through hell, keep going -------Winston Churchill

Self-care is how you take your power back.—Lalah Delia

Mental Health Assessment
(Check your answer)

1. Moving or speaking so slowly that it is noticeable to others or could have noticed. Even being so fidgety or restless that you have been moving around a lot more than usual.
   a. not at all _____
   b. Some days _____
   c. Majority of the day _____
   d. Nearly every day _____

2. Thoughts that no one cares for you, or you would be better off dead, or of self-mutilation/hurting yourself.
   a. not at all _____
   b. Some days _____
   c. Majority of the day _____
   d. Nearly every day _____

3. Feeling down depressed, without, empty, or hopeless
   a. not at all _____
   b. Some days _____
   c. Majority of the day _____
   d. Nearly every day _____

4. Trouble falling or staying asleep or sleeping too much.
   Poor appetite or overeating
   a. not at all _____
   b. Some days _____
   c. Majority of the day_____
   d. Nearly every day _____

5. Feeling bad about yourself or that you are a failure or have let yourself or your family down.
   a. not at all _____
   b. Some days _____
   c. Majority of the day _____
   d. Nearly every day _____

6. Trouble concentrating on things such as reading the newspaper or watching the telephone.
   a. not at all _____
   b. Some days _____
   c. Majority of the day _____
   d. Nearly every day _____

Total Not at all _____
Total Several Days _____
Total Majority of the day _____
Total Nearly every day _____

7. In the past week, I felt happier or more cheerful than usual
   a. Not at all
   b. Often
   c. Very Often
   d. Regularly
   e. All the time

8. In the past week, I have been more active than usual (either socially, sexually, at work, home, or school).
   a. Not at all
   b. Often
   c. Very Often
   d. Regularly
   e. All the time

9. Repeated, disturbing, and unwanted memories of the stressful experience?
    a. Not at all
    b. Somewhat
    c. Fairly
    d. Satisfactorily Much
    e. Majority of the time

10. Suddenly feeling or acting as if the stressful experience were happening again (as if you were back there reliving it)?
    a. Not at all
    b. Somewhat
    c. Fairly
    d. Satisfactorily Much
    e. Majority of the time

11. Feeling very upset when something reminds you of a stressful experience?
    a. Not at all
    b. Somewhat
    c. Fairly
    d. Satisfactorily Much
    e. Majority of the time

12. Having strong physical reactions when something reminds you of a stressful experience (for example, heart pounding, trouble breathing, sweating)?
    a. Not at all
    b. Somewhat
    c. Fairly
    d. Satisfactorily Much
    e. Majority of the time

13. Having strong negative beliefs about yourself, other people, or the world.
    a. Not at all
    b. Sometimes
    c. A Lot

14. Have any of your closest relationships been troubled by a lot of arguments or repeated breakups. (Check yes or no)
    a. Yes _____
    b. No _____

15. Have you deliberately hurt yourself physically (e.g., punched yourself, cut yourself, burned yourself)? How about making a suicide attempt? (Check yes or no)
    a. Yes _____
    b. No _____

16. Have you been extremely moody? (Check yes or no)
    a. Yes _____
    b. No _____

17. Have you felt very angry a lot of the time? How about often acting in an angry or sarcastic manner? (Check yes or no)
    a. Yes _____
    b. No _____

18. Recently, have there been times you were distrustful of others, more often than other times? (Check yes or no)
    a. Yes _____
    b. No _____

19. Lately have things seemed unreal or you felt unreal or numb? (Check yes or no)
    a. Yes _____
    b. No _____

20. Have you felt empty or like a strong void in your life? (Check yes or no)
    a. Yes _____
    b. No _____

21. Have there been times you had to wonder, "Who Am I"? (Check yes or no)
    a. Yes _____
    b. No _____

22. Have you found yourself talking to yourself? (Check yes or no)
    a. Yes _____
    b. No _____

23. Has others looked at you strange and you wondered what in the world
    are they looking at me for? (Check yes or no)
    a. Yes _____
    b. No _____

24. Do you feel that nobody loves you? (Check yes or no)
    a. Yes _____
    b. No _____

25. How do you feel about animals?
    a. Don't care about them.
    b. They are okay.
    c. Love them.
    d. Don't really know.

26. Who are you closest to? (Circle)

Mother	Father	Sister	Brother
Auntie	Uncle	Grandmother	Grandfather
Cousin	Friend	Pastor	Mentor
Counselor	Classmate	Teacher	Professor
Neighbor	Nobody	Boyfriend	Girlfriend
Stepmother	Stepfather	Need to thank about it	Not Sure
Comments:			

Anger management:

The goal of anger management is to minimize both your feelings and emotions, the physiological awakening that anger causes. You can't get rid of, or avoid, the things or the people that antagonize you, nor can you change them, but you can learn to control your reactions. Our hope is that you learn the necessary coping skills that you need to journey in a positive direction and to maintain, sustain and manage your anger. You will learn the three types of Anger: **Passive Aggression, Open Aggression, and Assertive Aggression**. We will talk about the five stages of Anger: **Trigger, Escalation, Crisis, Recovery, and Depression. Before discussing the three types of Anger, lets assess our FEELINGS.**

Learning to recognize and express anger appropriately can make a bid difference in your life.

FEELINGS CHECK: Simply identify your feelings at this time and write it here: _____

FEELINGS CHECK-IN

Excited	**Happy**	**Surprised**
Angry	**Sad**	**Scared**
Nervous	**Hurt**	**Proud**

TODAY I FEEL: _____

If you identify more than one identify them here:

1.	2.	3.		
4.	5.	6.		

Take each one of the feelings you have identified and discuss what those feelings means to you.

Your Feelings:

_____

Why are you feeling this way?

_____

_____

What cause you to feel this way?

_____

_____

_____

What are you doing to change this feeling?

_____

_____

_____

Are you Angry?

_____

_____

_____

If you are Angry, do you know Who you are Angry with?

_____

_____

_____

_____

How do you want to resolve this matter?

_____

_____

_____

_____

If there is someone you need to make amends, do you want to make amends?

_____

_____

_____

_____

_____

If no, why not?

_____

_____

_____

If you need to make amends, skip to pages 59-61 and then return back to this page after you complete "Making Amends" assignment.

_____

_____

_____

_____

_____

(PRE) TESTING YOUR ANGER CONTROL

1. I get angry with little or no provocation.
   1   2   3   4   5

2. I have a really bad temper.
   1   2   3   4   5

3. It's hard for me to let go of thoughts that make me angry.
   1   2   3   4   5

4. When I become angry, I have urges to beat someone up.
   1   2   3   4   5

5. When I become angry, I have urges to break or tear things.
   1   2   3   4   5

6. I get impatient when people don't understand me.
   1   2   3   4   5

7. I lose my temper at least once a week.
   1   2   3   4   5

8. I embarrass family, friends, or coworkers with my anger outbursts.
   1   2   3   4   5

9. I get impatient when people in front of me drive *exactly at* the speed limit.
   1   2   3   4   5

10. When my neighbors are inconsiderate, it makes me angry.
    1   2   3   4   5

11. I find myself frequently annoyed with certain friends or family.
    1   2   3   4   5

12. I get angry when people do things that they are not supposed to, like smoking in a no smoking section or having more items than marked in the supermarket express checkout line.

| 1 | 2 | 3 | 4 | 5 |

13. There are certain people who always rub me the wrong way.

| 1 | 2 | 3 | 4 | 5 |

14. I feel uptight/tense.

| 1 | 2 | 3 | 4 | 5 |

15. I yell and/or curse.

| 1 | 2 | 3 | 4 | 5 |

16. I get so angry I feel like I am going to explode with rage.

| 1 | 2 | 3 | 4 | 5 |

17. I get easily frustrated when machines/equipment do not work properly

| 1 | 2 | 3 | 4 | 5 |

18. I remember people and situations that made me angry for a long time.

| 1 | 2 | 3 | 4 | 5 |

19. I can't tolerate incompetence. It makes me angry.

| 1 | 2 | 3 | 4 | 5 |

20. I think people try to take advantage of me.

| 1 | 2 | 3 | 4 | 5 |

TOTAL: _____

Score Key:

80-100 Your anger expression is likely getting you into serious trouble with others. It would probably be worthwhile to seek professional help.

60-80 You may not need professional help but you need to work on controlling your anger in a very deliberate manner.

50-60 You have plenty of room for improvement. Reading a self help book on anger control could be beneficial.

30-50 You're probably getting angry as often as most people. Monitor your episodes of temper and see if you can lower your score in this test in 6 months.

Below 30- Congratulate yourself. You are likely in a good comfort zone.

Passive Aggression, Open Aggression, and Assertive Aggression.
Now let's discuss the three types of Anger.

- ## Passive Aggressive

  Passive-aggressive behavior is when one person is subtly aggressive towards another. This behavior aims to punish or retaliate to a perceived slight. A person exhibiting this behavior will use passive-aggressive actions rather than communicating their dissatisfaction with words. When you have been the target of this behavior, you may not realize that a person's hostility was purposeful. You may be left wondering why the person treated you poorly. Was it an accident? Are you being too sensitive?

- ## What are some of the reason people? behave passively aggressively?

1. Most of the time individuals use passive-aggressive behavior for different reasons. A person may not typically behave this way, but occasionally they will exhibit this behavior. According to clinical studies, Dr. B. Thomas Reddick, there are reasons why people act this way.

   - We are taught showing anger is intolerable.
   - Cover up or sugarcoated angry responses are welcome.
   - Aggressiveness is harder.
   - Trouble Free to rationalize behavior.
   - Getting Even feels superior.
   - Advantageous
   - Feel effective

Examples of Passive-Aggressive Behavior

Stubbornness, procrastination, and a get back behavior are typically exhibited. A person may false-face their anger by making excuses for their non-receptiveness. People who are confrontational or aggressive may deny being angry even though it is obvious that they are upset. A procrastinating passive-aggressive co-worker may wait until the last minute to complete their assigned work or submit work late as a means of getting back.

Passive Aggressive Speech

There are common ways that people speak to show their hidden unkindness. You may notice that the way they are talking to you doesn't quite make sense and that you are getting frustrated. According to clinical studies, passive-aggressive people may say:

- "I'm okay."
- "I'm not angry."
- "Okay"
- "Anyway"
- "I thought you knew."
- "I'd be delighted to."
- "I was only playing."
- "Why are you mad?"

Open Aggressive

Open aggression is a sharp contrast to passive-aggressive anger, as it's usually expressed outwardly---- mostly in a physically or verbally aggressive way. People who express outward anger often do so with the of hurting others or destroying things to retaliate for acts they perceived were wrongfully done to them.

Many people tend to lash out in anger and rage, becoming physically or verbally aggressive and can often hurt themselves or others. Open Aggression comes out in bullying, blackmailing, accusing, shouting, bickering, sarcasm, fighting, and criticism.

How to control your anger

1. Count to 10. Counting to 10 gives you time to cool down, so you can think more clearly and overcome the impulse to lash out.
2. Breathe slowly. ...
3. Inhale and Exhale
4. Exercise can help with anger. ...
5. Looking after yourself may keep you calm. ...
6. Get creative. ...
7. Talk about how you feel. ...
8. Anger management programs.
9. Méditation/Yoga/Payer/Read a Book etc.

• Assertive Agressive

Assertive anger: This is usually the best way to communicate feelings of anger because anger is expressed directly and in a nonthreatening way to the person involved. A statement such as "I feel angry when you ..." is an example of assertive anger.

We will talk about the five stages of Anger: Trigger, Escalation, Crisis, Recovery, and Depression.

Trigger:

Everyone has their own triggers for what makes them angry, but some common ones include situations in which we feel:

- Threatened or attacked.
- Frustrated or powerless
- Like we're being invalidated or treated unfairly
- Like people are not respecting our feelings or possessions.

Start by considering these 10 anger management tips.
a. Think before you speak.
b. Once you're calm, express your concerns.
c. Get some exercise.
d. Identify possible solutions.
e. Stick with "I" statements.
f. Don't hold a grudge.
g. Use humor to release tension.

Escalation:

Escalation. In this process, the escalation phase involves cues that indicate anger is building. As stated in the introduction to anger management, these cues can be physical, behavioral, emotional, or cognitive (thoughts). As you may recall, cues are warning signs, or responses, to anger-provoking events.

The Four-Step Verbal De-Escalation Process
- Step 1: Recognize and Assess the Situation. Your safety is paramount. ...
- Step 2: Respond Calmly. Human beings tend to mimic each other's behavior, so don't respond with anger, sarcasm, or inflexibility. ...
- Step 3: Listen with Empathy. ...
- Step 4: Validate and Show Respect.

Crisis:

The crisis phase involves the young person behaving in an aggressive manner, either physically or verbally, towards another person, an object or themselves. This may include shouting, throwing, or hitting an object and or striking a person.

Recovery:

Recovery is the physiological and psychological winddown phase that returns a young person to a pre-angry state. This slow cool down process can take from less than an hour to days, depending on the intensity and length of the anger-related episode.

Depression:

People with depressive illness often have symptoms of overt or suppressed anger. Can depression make you have anger issues?

Those with anger traits face exaggerated problems during symptomatic period of depression. Pharmacological management helps in control of depressive and anxiety symptoms, but rarely addresses anger symptoms.

Dealing with someone else's Anger:

Here are some tips:

Keep your cool. Don't answer anger with anger. Remember that anger can lead people to say things they don't really mean. Criticism, threats, or name-calling won't help resolve the situation. Don't take it personally. Try to understand why the person is angry. His or her feelings may have little or nothing to do with you. Listen to the person. Sometimes an angry person just needs to "blow off steam". Let the person express his or her feelings. Don't interrupt. Maintain eye contact to show you are listening. Think of solutions together. If you're having a conflict with someone, try to find solutions that you can both agree on. Do this only when you are both calm.

Some Common causes of anger to include, but not limited to:

1. **Stress:** Stress related to work, family, health, and money problems may make you feel anxious and irritable.

2. **Frustration/Resentment:** You may get angry if you fail to reach a goal or feel as if things are out of your control.

3. **Anxiety/Fear:** Anger is a natural response to threats of violence or to physical or verbal abuse.

4. **Aggravation/Annoyance:** You may reach in anger to minor irritations and daily hassles.

5. **Sadness/Disappointment:** Anger often results when expectations and desires aren't met.

6. **Bitterness/Resentment:** You may feel angry when you've been hurt, rejected, or offended.

MAKING AMENDS

Credit to Nick
https://www.amethystrecovery.org

As to Nick writing with Amethyst recovery & Dr. B. Thomas-Reddick believes that MAKING AMENDS is a vital part of an individual's life. When one understands the proper steps in how to make amends with people, they have either hurt or caused discomfort too, this allows one to fill the voids. Studies has proven that when an individual suffers with addictions one of the 12 steps that every Alcoholic Anonymous or Drug Disorder member needs to complete is rekindling with loved ones, family and friends. Not only does making amends help you get over past mistakes, but it also helps repair your relationships with other people. However, some people are afraid of making amends because they don't know what to say, how to start, or how others are going to respond. While everyone's journey is different, and you cannot control how others will respond, there are ways to approach this step appropriately.

Start With a Thoughtful Apology

When you make amends, you must apologize for the hurt and pain you caused. Keep in mind, it doesn't have to be a lengthy apology; it just needs to be honest. Some things you can open with include:

- I'm sorry.
- I feel bad about what I did.
- I'm sorry I made myself sick.

- I'm sorry for what I've put you through.
- I know this has been hard on both of us.

Take Responsibility for Your Actions

Don't deny responsibility for the harm you've caused, even if you think it was someone else's fault or the victim brought it to themselves. When making amends, owning the responsibility for your actions can sound like:

- I recognize I am powerless against drinking, or I recognize I am powerless against drugs.
- I accept responsibility for what I did.
- I know that I caused you harm.
- I acknowledge that I ignored your help.
- I realize that my actions were hurtful.

Admit What You Did Wrong

One of the most important parts of making amends is being specific about what you did wrong. Rather than saying something vague like, "I'm sorry for being rude to you," say something like, "When you were trying to introduce yourself at that party, I interrupted and made inappropriate comments, and I apologize for my behavior. Please accept my apology."

Don't try to justify what happened either; simply admit that your actions were wrong without explaining why they occurred in the first place. One way to recognize what you did wrong is by saying things like:

- I was wrong.
- I did this and I take full responsibility for my actions.
- This was my fault.

Genuinely Feel Remorse

It is important to genuinely feel remorse for the person you hurt, what you did, and the pain you caused. The person or people affected by your behavior are not even there in this room with you, so their feelings and reactions must come from within you. You need to be able to convey genuine feelings of remorse to make amends successfully.

Ask for Forgiveness

When asking for forgiveness, you must be sincere. This means that you are willing to accept the consequences of your actions. You also need to be ready to make amends and change your behavior in the future. If someone has forgiven you and is willing to accept your apology but continues to treat you poorly or speak badly about you to others, it's okay not to go back into their lives right away—but do try again eventually. Forgiveness works both ways, and sometimes, even though a person says they forgive you, they might not be ready to mean it yet.

Ask What You Can Do to Amend Your Wrongdoing

While it may seem like a simple question, the "What can I do?" question is more of a two-part query: First, you're asking permission to make amends. Second, what they say after they tell you what they need from you determines whether or not your apology has been accepted.

This is an important part of making amends because it shows that you're taking ownership of your actions. It lets others know that you're not going to repeat the same mistakes repeatedly by offering them a way to avoid having to deal with your apologies every week or two.

Be Patient and Persistent

If you're looking to make amends with a loved one or family member, you must take the time to develop a plan. You'll also want to be mindful of your intention and follow through on it consistently over time.

It can sometimes feel like an uphill battle when trying not just to apologize but also to make amends for past mistakes. But remember: the most important thing is that you do what's best for yourself and your relationship with this person in the long run, even if it takes smaller steps at first. So don't be afraid of asking for help from others in AA who might have more experience in this area than you.

It's important to remember that making amends is a process. You can't expect everything to go perfectly when you try to do it for the first time but keep trying. And even though you might still make some mistakes along the way, don't let them discourage you from making amends in future situations where appropriate.

(A Self Awareness Model)

"Who Are You?"

_____

Name

_____

DEMOGRAPHIC

Hopefully by now, you have read Dr. Barbara Reddick's book, The Presence of a Chaplain & My Personal Tapestry of Life. If you have not, we encourage you to also read as well.

This section will allow you to look at self to become aware of who you are and who you may want to become. Please read each question carefully and explain in detail your thoughts, feelings, concerns, and observations.

Please understand that this is your personal tapestry of life and only you will read it unless you decide to share as I have. The journey in this student handbook will hopefully allow you to become empowered with your self-awareness. Work at your own pace, realizing that you can stop and start at any time.

(If you feel uncomfortable answering any of the questions, move on to the next question until you complete it. At the end of the journey, you may feel comfortable revisiting the unanswered questions.)

NAME:

DATE:

TIME:

AGE:

✓ EDUCATION

7th	8th	9th	10th	11th	12th	1 yr college	2 yr college	3 yr college	4 yr college	5 yr college	6 yr college

Male: _____c

Female: _____

✓ Please (How many children do you have?)

- ○ Married   Children: 1-2   3-4   5-6   7-8   9-10
- ○ Divorce
- ○ Single
- ○ Dating
- ○ Student

Share how you are feeling at this moment. (In detail)

_____
_____
_____
_____
_____
_____
_____
_____
_____
_____
_____
_____
_____
_____
_____
_____
_____

_____

_____

_____

Do you have a clue of what you would like to learn about yourself?
YES _____   NO _____

Explain what you would like to learn about YOU?

_____

_____

_____

_____

_____

_____

_____

_____

_____

What is your favorite food? _____						
What is your favorite game you like to play? _____						
What do you like to do? _____						
Who is your favorite Artist? _____						
What grade are you presently in? _____						
What is your favorite sport? _____						
If you could meet a celebrity, who would you choose?_____						
WHO RAISED YOU?						
Mother	Father	Grandma	Grandpa	Sister	Brother	Auntie
Other Family	Uncle	Pastor	Friends	Neighbors	Teacher	Cousin or Other

WHAT IS YOUR FAVORITE COLOR?

Do you have a pet, if so, share the name?

_____
_____
_____

_____
_____
_____

If you have a pet, describe the level of care you provide for your pet.

_____
_____
_____

How many pets have you had in your lifetime? _____

From a scale from 1 to 10, how would you number yourself as the level of care for pets? 1---don't care at all for pets 10--- care a whole lot

_____

Do you attend church? (Do not have to answer)
YES _____ NO _____

If you attend church, temple, or synagogue? What is your denomination?

_____
_____
_____

What do you like about your church, temple, or synagogue?

_____
_____
_____

What would You like to be when you grow up?

_____

_____

_____

How many siblings do you have? (circle)

1	2	3	4	5	6	7	8	9	10

How many stepsisters or step brothers do you have?

1	2	3	4	5	6	7	8	9	10

Do you like school? If no, explain why.

_____

_____

_____

_____

_____

_____

_____

_____

_____

If you like school, explain in detail what you like about school and why?

_____

_____

_____

_____

_____

_____

_____

_____

While growing up who raised you? Explain this experience.

_____

_____

_____

_____

_____

_____

_____

_____

Are you okay with who raised you? If yes explain, if no explain.

_____

_____

_____

_____

_____

_____

_____

_____

How was your upbringing? Explain

_____

_____

_____

_____

_____

_____

_____

_____

_____

_____

_____

_____

_____

_____

_____

_____

_____

Paint the picture in words how you would like for your family to look.

_____

_____

_____

_____

_____

_____

_____

_____

If you could change one thing about your family lifestyle, what would it be?

_____

_____

_____

_____

_____

_____

_____

_____

_____

_____

Are you being raised by both parents, single parent, or no parent, etc.? Explain

_____

_____

_____

_____

_____

_____

_____

_____

Which parent do you feel comfortable to share your deep thoughts with?
Mom _____ Dad ___ Other_____

Who is your favorite teacher and why?

_____
_____
_____
_____
_____
_____
_____
_____

What is it you like about this teacher?

_____
_____
_____

If you could change one thing in your school, what would it be?

_____
_____
_____
_____
_____
_____
_____
_____

Do you like your school that you are presently attending?

_____
_____
_____

If yes, why, if no why?

YES: _____

_____

_____

_____

_____

_____

NO: _____

_____

_____

_____

_____

While growing up, did you spend time with grandma and grandpa?

_____

_____

_____

_____

_____

_____

_____

_____

_____

If you spent time with either, explain how you felt then and now?

_____

_____

_____

_____

_____

_____

_____

_____

_____

If you did not spend time with your grandparents, how do you feel about this?

_____

_____

_____

_____

_____

_____

_____

Do you feel that there are benefits for children who have grandparents in their lives? If so, why? If not, why?

_____

_____

_____

_____

_____

See how you are feeling NOW.

_____

_____

_____

_____

_____

Do you feel that this student handbook is helping you thus far?
YES _____ NO _____

Express how this student handbook is helping you thus far.

1.

_____
_____
_____
_____

2.

_____
_____
_____
_____

3.

_____
_____
_____
_____

What do you enjoy doing when you have free time?

_____
_____
_____
_____

What are your strengths?

_____
_____
_____

What are your weaknesses?

_____
_____
_____
_____

If you could change one thing about you, what would it be and why?

_____

_____

_____

_____

_____

_____

_____

If there is something you could change, do you feel that this has hindered you from moving forward in your life?

_____

_____

_____

_____

_____

_____

_____

_____

_____

_____

_____

_____

Do you feel that life hasn't been fair?
YES _____ NO _____

EXPLAIN:

_____
_____
_____

_____
_____

_____
_____
_____

_____
_____

_____
_____

_____
_____

_____
_____
_____

_____
_____

_____

If you feel that life for you hasn't been fair, identify one thing you can do to move things forward in a positive manner.

_____

_____

_____

_____

_____

_____

_____

_____

Name one thing that you really dislike for someone to say or do to you?

_____

_____

_____

_____

_____

_____

_____

_____

Is there someone you are angry with? _____ Yes or ____ No

_____

If there is someone you are angry with, why?

_____

_____

_____

_____

_____

Have you tried to resolve this matter?
YES _____ NO _____

Do you want to resolve the matter if it is not resolved currently? If yes, how do you plan on putting this behind you?

_____

_____

_____

_____

_____

_____

_____

_____

_____

ACTIVITY

TAKE TIME TO WRITE A LETTER TO SOME ONE
YOU WANT TO MAKE AMENDS WITH!
THERE MAY BE MORE THAN ONE PERSON.
USING THE NEXT FORMAT or YOU CAN USE YOUR PAPER.

FROM: _____
_____
_____

TO:_____
_____
_____

Dear _____:
_____
_____
_____

_____
_____
_____

_____
_____
_____

_____
_____
_____

Sincerely,

TAKE A BREAK!!!!!!!
Debrief

Self-Care

Embrace the moment of your true feelings and know that if you are feeling angry, mad, happy, sad, or some anxiety, it's okay.

Examples of taking a break:

1. Take a walk!
2. Drink a cup of coffee or hot tea etc.
3. Inhale/Exhale
4. Yoga/Exercise
5. Meditation/Prayer
6. Self-Care

WELCOME BACK!!!!!!

TAKE AN OBSERVATION OF HOW YOU ARE FEELING AT THIS TIME.

_____
_____
_____
_____
_____
_____
_____
_____
_____
_____
_____
_____
_____
_____
_____
_____
_____
_____
_____

External and Internal Alterations

Have you ever used drugs?
Yes _____ No _____

Have you ever used alcohol?
Yes _____ No _____

If yes, what type of drug have you ever used?

If not, explain on a separate sheet of paper, sharing a moment in your life where you wanted to use but didn't.

_____
_____
_____

_____
_____
_____

_____
_____
_____

_____
_____
_____

What kept you from using it?

_____

_____

_____

_____

_____

_____

Share this experience of how this make you feel that you were able to not use drugs or alcohol.

_____

_____

_____

_____

_____

_____

_____

Cannabis _____ Heroin _____ Cocaine _____ Crack Cocaine ___
Hallucinogen _____ Ecstasy _____ Methamphetamine
_____Molly_____Flakka_____Alcohol_____

_____Fentanyl

Please explain the age you started using drugs. _____

Who introduced drugs to you? _____

How do you feel about this person today?

_____

_____

_____

_____

_____

_____

Did you trust this person at the time he or she introduced this drug to you?

_____
_____
_____
_____
_____
_____
_____
_____
_____
_____

What would you do differently if you could turn back the hands of time?

_____
_____
_____
_____
_____
_____
_____
_____
_____
_____
_____
_____
_____

How do you feel about leaders?

_____
_____
_____
_____
_____
_____
_____
_____
_____

How do you feel a leader should lead?

_____
_____
_____
_____
_____
_____
_____
_____
_____
_____
_____

If you attend church, temple, or synagogue, how do you feel about your pastor, rabbi, or priest, etc.?

_____

_____

_____

_____

_____

_____

_____

_____

_____

_____

Does your pastor, rabbi, priest, etc., exemplify good leadership skills?

_____

_____

_____

_____

_____

_____

_____

_____

_____

_____

_____

If not, identify the areas you would like your leader to improve in.

_____

_____

_____

_____

_____

_____

_____

_____

_____

_____

Define leadership.

_____

_____

_____

_____

_____

_____

_____

_____

_____

_____

_____

_____

How do you feel about this overall observation of self and others?

_____

_____

_____

_____

_____

_____

_____

_____

_____

_____

_____

_____

_____

_____

_____

_____

_____

Would you recommend this workbook to someone else?
Yes _____   No _____

GREAT WORK!!! YOU DESERVE A PAT ON THE BACK. I look forward to speaking with you soon. We can arrange for a conference call if you'd like.

Dr. Barbara Thomas-Reddick

WHEN YOU DO NOT KNOW WHO YOU ARE, YOU WILL BE WHAT OTHERS WANT YOU TO BE!!!

"WHO ARE YOU?"

_____

_____

_____

WHEN YOU COMPLETE YOUR HANDBOOK, IN ORDER TO RECEIVE YOUR CERTIFICATE OF COMPLETION, CONTACT Dr. Barbara Thomas-Reddick at 850-201-7105 Office/ 850-201-7101 Fax or email me at Holisticplanofcare@gmail.com

IF YOU WOULD LIKE TO BOOK DR. BARBARA THOMAS- REDDICK FOR FUTURE ENGAGEMENTS FEEL FREE TO CONTACT ME AT THE NUMBER ABOVE.

WEBSITE:
www.thepresenceofachaplain.com
WWW.HPOCARE.ORG
www.ifgoddontdoit.com

Stay focused for upcoming book on PARENTING.

LET'S TAKE A POST ANGER TEST AND COMPARE THE TWO.

(POST) TESTING YOUR ANGER CONTROL

1. I get angry with little or no provocation.
   1   2   3   4   5

2. I have a really bad temper.
   1   2   3   4   5

3. It's hard for me to let go of thoughts that make me angry.
   1   2   3   4   5

4. When I become angry, I have urges to beat someone up.
   1   2   3   4   5

5. When I become angry, I have urges to break or tear things.
   1   2   3   4   5

6. I get impatient when people don't understand me.
   1   2   3   4   5

7. I lose my temper at least once a week.
   1   2   3   4   5

8. I embarrass family, friends, or coworkers with my anger outbursts.
   1   2   3   4   5

9. I get impatient when people in front of me drive *exactly at* the speed limit.
   1   2   3   4   5

10. When my neighbors are inconsiderate, it makes me angry.
    1   2   3   4   5

11. I find myself frequently annoyed with certain friends or family.
    1   2   3   4   5

12. I get angry when people do things that they are not supposed to, like smoking in a no smoking section or having more items than marked in the supermarket express checkout line.

1   2   3   4   5

13. There are certain people who always rub me the wrong way.

1   2   3   4   5

14. I feel uptight/tense.

1   2   3   4   5

15. I yell and/or curse.

1   2   3   4   5

16. I get so angry I feel like I am going to explode with rage.

1   2   3   4   5

17. I get easily frustrated when machines/equipment do not work properly

1   2   3   4   5

18. I remember people and situations that made me angry for a long time.

1   2   3   4   5

19. I can't tolerate incompetence. It makes me angry.

1   2   3   4   5

20. I think people try to take advantage of me.

1   2   3   4   5

TOTAL: _____

Score Key:

80-100 Your anger expression is likely getting you into serious trouble with others. It would probably be worthwhile to seek professional help.

60-80 You may not need professional help, but you need to work on controlling your anger in a very deliberate manner.

50-60 You have plenty of room for improvement. Reading a self-help book on anger control could be beneficial.

30-50 You're probably getting angry as often as most people. Monitor your episodes of temper and see if you can lower your score in this test in 6 months.

Below 30- Congratulate yourself. You are likely in a good comfort zone.

Final Test for completion

Name the Four Parenting Styles:

1. _____

2. _____

3. _____

4. _____

Describe your Style of Parenting:

_____

_____

_____

Would you prefer another parenting style?

(Check one)

a. yes_____

b. no_____

Name a warning sign that a parent may be too strict.

_____

1. **Who is the Professor for this class?**
   a. Joyce Melanie
   b. Dr. Roy Lee
   c. Dr. Barbara Thomas-Reddick

2. **Define Anger**
   a. a strong feeling of annoyance, displeasure, or hostility
   b. Anger can be a good thing. It can give you a way to express negative feelings, for example, or motivate you to find solutions to problems.
   c. It is okay to be angry, it is what you do with it.
   d. All above

3. **Write down the three types of Anger?**
   1. _____
   2. _____
   3. _____

4. **Learning to recognize and express anger appropriately can make a bid difference in your life.**
   True or False (circle)

5. **The Five Stages of Anger.**
   a. _____   b. _____
   c. _____   d. _____
   e. _____

6. **Mental health includes our:**
   a. emotional well-being
   b. psychological well-being
   c. social well-being
   d. ALL OF THE ABOVE

7. **Mental health is important at**
   a. the end of live
   a. at every state of live
   a. at the beginning of the situation
   b. ALL OF THE ABOVE

8. Mental health is important because it can help you to:
    a. Cope with the stresses of live
    b. Seek more jobs to do
    c. Have a good relationship
    d. Be physically healthy
    e. Make meaningful contributions to your community
    f. a, c, d, e

9. Mental health affects how we:
    a. think, feel and act
    b. how we attend church
    c. what job we choose

10. From a scale from 1-10, (1 being not so good, 10 being doing great), how would you rate your mental status at this time? _____

AFTER YOU HAVE COMPLETED THE CLASS WITH A 70% or higher, YOU WILL RECEIVE A CERTIFICATE OF COMPLETION IN YOUR EMAIL. SIGNED BY Dr. Barbara Thomas-Reddick or another Holistic Plan of Care Member. (HPOC)

HOLISTIC PLAN OF CARE, INCORPORATED

N A M E

S HERE NOW RECOGNIZED FOR SUCESSFUL COMPLETION

Of the

MENTAL HEALTH CLASS

On

DATE

_____

CEO/FACILITATOR/Certified Addiction Professional

Printed in the United States
by Baker & Taylor Publisher Services